Fountains
of Philadelphia

For Bell Brady

Enjoy exploring our
wonderful fountains. Happy
Splashing

Jim McClelland

Fountains
of Philadelphia

A GUIDE

Jim McClelland

STACKPOLE
BOOKS

To Lynn H. Miller,
who encouraged me in this project from the beginning
and always found time to listen, to encourage,
to improve, and to act as my in-house editor.

Copyright ©2005 by Stackpole Books

Published by
STACKPOLE BOOKS
5067 Ritter Rd.
Mechanicsburg PA 17055
www.stackpolebooks.com

Printed in China

10 9 8 7 6 5 4 3 2 1

FIRST EDITION

Photographs by the author unless noted below
    Craig A. Benner iv, xii, 22 (both), 24 (top), 25, 26, 39 (both), 40, 49, 56 (bottom)
    Pete Checchia 56 (top)
    Fairmount Park Commission Archives 24 (bottom)
    Longwood Gardens 68, 70, 71, 72
    Paul W. Meyer 64 (bottom), 65
    Nemours Mansion and Gardens i, 78

Cover design by Wendy Reynolds

Cover: Voyage of Ulysses Fountain
Page i: Cherub with Turtles Fountain at Nemours Gardens
Page ii: LOVE Park Fountain

Library of Congress Cataloging-in-Publication Data

McClelland, Jim.
    Fountains of Philadelphia : a guide / Jim McClelland.–1st ed.
        p.   cm.
    ISBN 0-8117-3191-X (pbk.)
    1. Fountains–Pennsylvania–Philadelphia.   I. Title.
NA9410.P48M38   2005
714–dc22   2004008836

Contents

Foreword

STANDING OUTSIDE PHILADELPHIA'S ORNATE CITY HALL ON A SUNNY JUNE day, a visitor can look down Benjamin Franklin Parkway toward the Philadelphia Museum of Art and see the transformative power of water.

In the foreground, a column thrusts up from a frothing pool at JFK Plaza, echoing the tower of City Hall directly across the street. Farther away, at Logan Circle, a slender jet rises from Alexander Stirling Calder's Swann Memorial Fountain, with falling arcs of water. In the far distance, about a mile and down the parkway, an even more delicate jet of water traces its course on the plaza fronting the great neoclassical museum.

These columns of water echo each other. Framed by sycamores running the length of the boulevard, they serve as markers of place, reminders that whatever else cities may be, they are works of craft—beautiful, evocative, reflective. A road that would otherwise serve only as an autobahn cutting to the heart of the city is redeemed by its fountains and public art and so retains a measure of its intended stately beauty.

Fountains are a measure of a city's humanity and imagination. They are created by artists, artisans, and laborers, often for a very specific time and place. Once they are installed and shimmering or splashing, people are drawn to them, sometimes falling in.

◀ CURTIS CENTER FOUNTAIN

Fountains soften what might otherwise be a harsh plaza and make it inviting or, in the case of JFK Plaza, more memorable. Fountains lure people into taking risks—as anyone who has attempted to get to Swann Fountain from the wrong place well knows. Fountains mark arrivals and departures, like the pool set in the art museum courtyard.

Philadelphia has many examples of these wonderful creations. What is remarkable is that no one has chosen to write about them. Fortunately, Jim McClelland has now rectified that sad situation. We are all happier for his effort.

At the same time, McClelland's work suggests how difficult the life of a fountain may be. For one thing, fountains are expensive. In fact, not too long ago, a fountain was the contemporary centerpiece of Independence Mall, the open expanse sweeping north from Independence Hall. But after only a few years of operation, the Judge Edwin O. Lewis Memorial Fountain—a monumental display honoring the man whose single-minded efforts led to the creation of Independence Park and the mall half a century ago—broke down completely. It was deemed too costly to repair and was finally designed into oblivion during the most recent makeover of the mall, now almost complete.

Many fountains around the city are not operating. Most, if not all of these are publicly owned, which means that repair and maintenance are subject to the increasingly stretched public purse.

But privately owned fountains also lead occasionally problematic existences. Not too many years ago, Philadelphia nearly lost one of its great works of art when the owners of Dream Garden, a monumental mosaic and fountain in the lobby of the Curtis Building off Washington Square, sought to sell the mosaic to a private collector. The city, with broad public support, managed to stop that sale and Dream Garden remains where its artist collaborators, Louis Tiffany and Maxfield Parrish, intended it to remain. Fountains are pools of memory and now visitors can contemplate the near loss of this great work when they visit Dream Garden—as Jim McClelland urges them to do.

Stephan Salisbury
Philadelphia Inquirer
Staff Cultural Writer

Maps

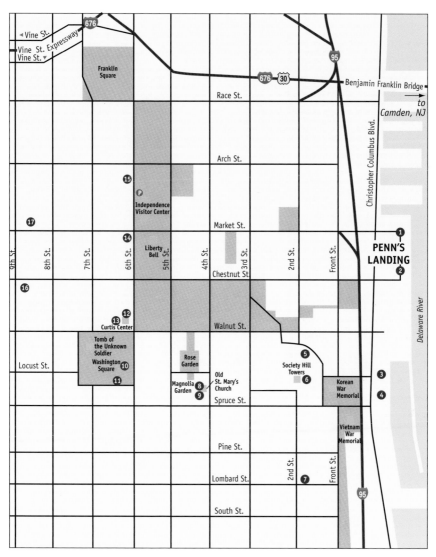

1. Great Plaza Fountain I
2. Great Plaza Fountain II
3. Five Water Spouts
4. Sphere Fountain
5. Una Biforcazione
   e Tre Paesaggi
6. Society Hill Towers
   Plaza Fountain
7. Head House Square
   Fountain
8. Magnolia Garden I
9. Magnolia Garden II
10. Washington Square
    Fountain
11. Hopkinson House
12. Dream Garden Fountain
13. Curtis Center Court
    Fountain
14. Milkweed Pod Fountain
15. Ulysses Fountain
16. Ben Franklin House
    Lobby Fountain
17. Gallery Fountains

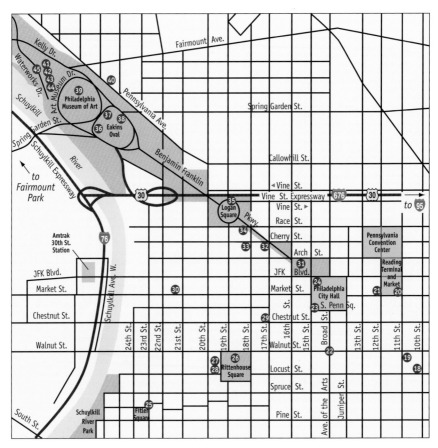

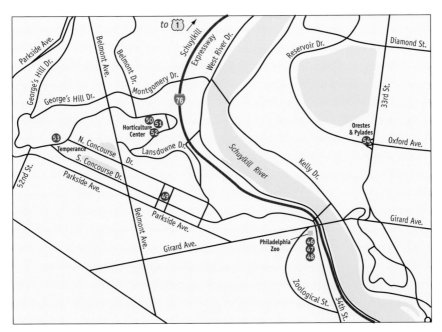

Preface

ANCIENT ROME HAD ITS LEGENDARY BATHS. GARDENS AND QUIET POOLS OF water surround the Taj Mahal, one of the world's most beautiful buildings, reflecting its bulbous dome and slender minarets.

The Alhambra, a renowned Moorish fortress-palace in Spain, uses water as an integral feature in its design. In its Court of Myrtles, a great placid pond mirrors Comares Tower at the far end. And in its Court of Lions is the famous marble and alabaster fountain.

Paris has its renowned Place de la Concorde fountains, made even more famous to moviegoers in the 1950s by their central inclusion in the musical film *An American in Paris*.

And Rome, with its myriad of waterworks, is called the City of Fountains.

Rome's sister city could be Philadelphia, which is also a City of Fountains, although few tourists see these wonderful works of water. Most Philadelphians can name the Swann Fountain on Logan Square (probably the most glorious) and the Washington Monument in front of the Philadelphia Museum of Art on the Benjamin Franklin Parkway, but they may be hard-pressed to name other fountains. That may be because both residents and tourists alike know the city for its historical significance, rather than its fountains.

◀ SWANN MEMORIAL FOUNTAIN

This book is intended to stimulate you to want to explore these fountains and come to know the watery beauty of Philadelphia. *Fountains of Philadelphia* gives both visitors and residents information on how to find the city's wonders of water, historical details, and facts about their design and structure.

Thanks go to the Philadelphia City Council for passing the trailblazing "percent for art" ordinance in 1959, making Philadelphia the first municipality in America to mandate that a percentage of construction costs for city projects be set aside for the fine arts. That same year, the Redevelopment Authority established an unprecedented program that requires developers to allocate one percent of their construction costs for the fine arts.

This book is designed by neighborhoods within the city, as well as areas near Philadelphia. Most outdoor fountains are working only in the months of good weather—spring through fall. For the most part, those fountains located within the city are more or less in walking distance of one another, other than in Fairmount Park, where transportation is required. Take your time and enjoy the city's splashes of liquid meditation.

IN THE TIME THAT I HAVE SPENT ON THE RESEARCH AND WRITING OF THIS book, I have been blessed by the friendship and support of a great many people. Administrators and staff at many organizations gave generously of their time, advice, and expertise; I am grateful for the opportunity to acknowledge and thank some of them here.

They include Matthew K. Holliday, Editor, *Pennsylvania Magazine*, which is where this project first started; Steve Lynch, who shared his rare nineteenth-century books on Philadelphia with me; John Barry Kelly, Maintenance Department, Independence National Park, for sharing his wealth of knowledge on the Catholic Abstinence Fountain; Robert Linck, Philadelphia Fountain Society; Tim Braxton, Assistant Manager, Hopkinson House Condominium; Ginette Meluso, Media Manager, Philadelphia Zoo; Christine Pape, Marketing Coordinator, the Morris Arboretum; Susan Matson, Collections Coordinator, Nemours Mansion and Gardens; Robert G. Martin, Director, Property Management, Atlantic American Properties; Nancy Robinson, I. M. Pei, Architect; Michael De Santo, Fairmount Park Facilities Manager; Penny Balkin Bach, Executive Director, and Laura Griffeth, Assistant Director, Fairmount Park Art Association; Craig A. Benner and Pete Checchia, Photographers; Richard

McClure, Manager, Kennedy Wilson Properties; Emily Smith, Friends of Rittenhouse Square; and Gail H. Fahrer, the Barra Foundation.

I also thank several librarians, archivists, and research specialists who provided materials I needed and cooperated and patiently answered my questions: Theresa Stuhlman, Archivist, Fairmount Park Commission Archives; Alessandro Pezzati, Archivist, the University Museum of the University of Pennsylvania; and Paul Steinke, Chairman, Preservation Alliance of Greater Philadelphia. A special thanks to Colvin Randall, Public Relations Manager, Longwood Gardens, for sharing his vast library with me.

Finally, to Kyle R. Weaver, Editor, Stackpole Books, for seeing the value in this book from the start, and to Amy Cooper, Managing Editor at Stackpole, who greatly assisted in the selection of photographs.

The Fairmount Waterworks

In 1812, Philadelphia began to build a new waterworks at "Fair Mount," near Morris Hill. A series of graceful buildings arose, with slender columns and wide terraces fronting on the Schuylkill River. The new works became a classic example of the Greek Revival style of the early nineteenth century and were called by some critics "the Athens of America."

The city's mid-nineteenth-century gentrification, especially in the Rittenhouse Square area, gave its residents living in Victorian mansions—as well as the rest of the city's residents—ample opportunity, particularly on weekends, to take advantage of promenading through Fairmount Park and the Waterworks' lovely pathways.

The Fairmount Waterworks was the nation's first large-scale municipal waterworks, and a phenomenon in its time. This ensemble of buildings, constructed over a sixty-year period, is one of the finest examples of Neoclassical architecture in the United States. Frederick Graff, and later his son, Frederick Jr., designed, engineered, and modified the structures and their machinery over the nearly one hundred years the site supplied Philadelphia's drinking water. Graff became the leading American expert on hydraulic engineering, and as a result of his local success, he was called upon for advice by New York when it installed its Croton water system in 1842, and by Boston in 1848.

In its day, the Waterworks concept was simple yet revolutionary: take upstream water (thought to be cleaner) from the Schuylkill; pump it up to a reservoir, built where the Art Museum now stands; and let pipes carry it downhill, bringing water to a rapidly growing city.

The water began flowing in 1815, and the spectacle drew sightseers from across the United States and Europe. In 1840, Charles Dickens came to look and later wrote: "The Waterworks, which are on a height near the city, are no less ornamental than useful, being tastefully laid out as a public garden, and kept in the best and neatest order. The river is dammed at this point, and forced by its own power into certain high tanks or reservoirs, whence the whole city, to the top stories of the houses, is supplied at a very trifling expense."

But factories and sewage began to pollute the water supply, forcing the city to turn to sand filtration system beds for purification. The Waterworks became obsolete, and closed in 1909. But in 1911, City Council passed a resolution decreeing that "the beautiful buildings" should be "preserved for all times."

In 1911, nearly all the equipment was replaced with fish tanks, and the Philadelphia Aquarium opened to the public on Thanksgiving Day, becoming one of the four largest in the world. One tank was 30 feet long, the largest anywhere. The state legislature provided the tanks, and the Pennsylvania State Fish and Game and the Forestry Protective Association supplied the finances and the fish. It was popular in its time, but it closed in December 1962 because of declining audiences and lack of maintenance funding.

In the following years, the site was declared a historic and engineering landmark, but it remained empty. In 1974, the Junior League led a fund-raising campaign for the site's restoration, but the funds raised were inadequate to get the work off the ground. By the 1980s, it was clear something had to be done to keep the rotting buildings from falling into the river, so the $7.8 million that had been raised during the 1970s was spent to reinforce the structures.

Another group of concerned citizens came forward in the early 1990s to spearhead the continuing fund-raising effort. After a Herculean effort to rescue the iconic, nineteenth-century engineering marvel, the renovation of the almost 190-year-old Waterworks was completed. It had taken thirty years and was finished at a cost of $30 million from a mix of private donations and public funding. All details of the restoration are painstakingly historic, from the shade of paint to the 1870s-style lighting fixtures.

With the Fairmount Waterworks, Philadelphia built a temple to industry that was a public attraction from the beginning and became the genesis of the extensive Fairmount Park system. To visit Philadelphia without seeing Fairmount and the Waterworks, it once was said, was like visiting London without seeing Westminster Abbey.

Also on the grounds, just beyond the Waterworks, in the South Garden, is the **Peace Fountain,** erected to commemorate the end of the Civil War. Below the trefoil arch is inscribed, PEACE JUNE 1865. More than 7 feet tall, the Peace Fountain is an important feature in the landscape. It is a historic structure that contributes to the aesthetics of the site and provides insight into the life of tourists in the nineteenth century, when it provided clean drinking water to refresh visitors. In the same vicinity is the **Marble Fountain,** one of the earliest installations in the South Garden. The first mention of planting in this garden occurred in 1830. Shortly thereafter, construction of the Marble Fountain began. Built between 1832 and 1833, the large, circular fountain was powered by an adjacent reservoir and became the focal point of the

▼ MARBLE FOUNTAIN

▲ PEACE FOUNTAIN

South Garden. The sculpture atop the basin was originally *Boy And Dolphin,* but it was replaced in 1832 by William Rush's bronze *Allegory of the Schuylkill River,* also called *Water Nymph and Bittern.* The central jet reached 25 feet and could be seen from across the river.

Also on these grounds is a memorial to Frederick Graff Sr., who designed the landscaped gardens surrounding the Waterworks. Frederick K. Graff Jr. became one of Philadelphia's leading civil engineers and led the movement to develop Fairmount Park to protect the Schuylkill River from pollution. Although the bust of Graff is commonly attributed to William Rush, it was actually carved in 1847, a decade after Rush's death. According to a contract in 1847, the design was to be executed by John Struthers and Son. The Graff Memorial, the Peace Fountain, and the Marble Fountain are all in a state of disrepair, but as of this writing, funds have been raised to restore this trio.

Today Fairmount Park, starting at the Waterworks, is the largest municipal park in the world, with more than 9,000 acres containing beautiful recreation complexes and some of Philadelphia's greatest historic and cultural treasures for residents and visitors to enjoy year-round. The Waterworks is

▼ LION'S HEAD DRINKING FOUNTAIN

now designated a U.S. National Historic Landmark and a National Historic Mechanical and Civil Engineering Landmark.

Dr. Wilson Cary Swann established the Philadelphia Fountain Society in 1869. Believing that the lack of water for workers and animals led to intemperance and crime, the society provided fountains and watering troughs throughout the city and park so that workers could quench their thirst in public instead of entering local taverns.

By the time the society undertook the construction of the **Swann Memorial Fountain** (see p. 21) in 1920, Prohibition and the mass production of the automobile had considerably reduced the society's activity. The Swann Fountain was the society's final splash. It turned a humane and moral mission to provide water into a celebration, immortalizing itself through its gift to the future.

Just as Fairmount Park was originally developed to protect and preserve the city's water supply—the Schuylkill River—drinking fountains were erected over natural springs so that citizens of Philadelphia could have an even more abundant supply of drinking water.

▼ LEMON HILL DRINKING FOUNTAIN

▲ WILLIAM LEONIDAS DRINKING FOUNTAIN

The park's springs provided an important alternative source of water for Philadelphians for many years. People's cars lined the park drives while they gathered to fill as many bottles as they could carry with fresh water. Urban encroachment necessitated their closure in 1961, but they remain attractive ornaments and artifacts of an earlier time. At their peak, approximately ninety of these springs were in use. Today about thirty-five can still be seen.

Illustrated here are several drinking fountains, springs, and watering troughs that can still be found, although their waters have been silenced.

Fairmount Park

AN ACT OF THE GENERAL ASSEMBLY DATED MARCH 26, 1867, APPROVED THE boundaries of Fairmount Park and invested title and ownership in the city of Philadelphia. It further stated that the city was empowered to "appropriate and set apart forever the area of land and water comprised within the limits . . . as open public ground and Park for the preservation of Schuylkill water and of the health and enjoyment of the people forever."

From the minutes of a meeting of the Commissioners of Fairmount Park in 1868:

> The ground we propose to acquire is peculiarly adapted to Park purposes. No other city in the Union has within its boundaries, streams which, in picturesque and romantic beauty, can compare with the Wissahickon and the Schuylkill; and there are few which include within their limits landscapes which, in sylvan grace and beauty, surpass those which abound within the spaces we propose to appropriate. Nature herself has so adorned them that little remains for art to do except skillfully develop the natural beauties of the ground. Here through long coming generations . . . will this park continue—a monument of wisdom and the foresight of those who founded it—protecting the purity and securing the abundance of their water supply; ministering in its clear air and ample grounds to their health and enjoyment and in the beauty and grace of its natural and its artificial adornments to the refinement of their

◀ FOUNTAIN OF THE SEA HORSES

taste; while to the spots already of historic interest, which are within its bounds, will be added others on which stately buildings will arise, for works of art or taste, or for instruction in natural science, or where monuments will be reared to the immortal memory of those who in their day have greatly served the State.

Thus was Fairmount Park born.

After leaving the Waterworks, you will discover the **Fountain of the Sea Horses,** just a few steps away. This playful water and statuary creation, designed by German sculptor Christopher Untenberger, was a gift to the city of Philadelphia from the Italian government in 1928 in commemoration of the Sesquicentennial of American Independence. Four equine travertine marble beauties are the focal point of this wonderful fountain, which reaches a total height of nearly 10 feet and has a pool that is 155 feet in circumference. This is a replica of the Fontana Dei Cavalli in the Borghese Gardens in Rome, c. 1740.

Drive back in front of the Art Museum to West River Drive for a visit to America's first zoo, the Philadelphia Zoological Gardens, at 34th and West Girard Avenue. Signs clearly mark the way. Pick up a map at the gate when

you enter. Here you will find 42 beautiful acres with more than sixteen hundred animals in a Victorian setting. Just inside the main entrance, you will see a wonderful, re-created three-tiered, cast-iron **Victorian Fountain,** built in 1984.

Not far from there, in front of the Rare Animal Conservation Center, is the wonderful **Impala Fountain.** This 20-foot-high sculpture was designed by Henry Mitchell (1915–80) and sits in a pool 68 by 34 feet. Twelve streamlined bronze impalas are caught in flight from an unknown predator, leaping high over ten jets of water in a black granite fountain, while a mother impala

◀ VICTORIAN FOUNTAIN

and calf stand nearly, apparently unaware of any danger. The skeletal forms are characteristic of the impala's lightness and agility, and they are executed in three graceful arcs. The fountain is dedicated to the memory of Herbert C. Morris, a former officer and director of the zoo. Most of the cost of the $140,000 project was donated by Mrs. Morris and the Fairmount Park Art Association. The bronze animals were cast by Battaglia and Company in Milan, and the fountain was dedicated on April 25, 1964. Henry Mitchell was a native of Ohio and became one of Philadelphia's best-known animal sculptors. More of his works can be found around Philadelphia.

Farther into the zoo, look for the picnic grove at the south end of the grounds, and enjoy the high-spouting **Picnic Grove Fountain** in the center. This fountain was part of a refurbishment to the picnic area in 1986.

When you leave the zoo, head toward Memorial Hall on North Concourse Drive. This impressive building is one of the few structures left from the Centennial Exhibition of 1876. For years, the Fairmount Park Association had its offices in the building. In the near future, it will be the home of the Please Touch Children's Museum. Just across from Memorial Hall is the **John Welsh Memorial Fountain** and Garden, dedicated to John Welsh (1805–86) for

▲ PICNIC GROVE FOUNTAIN

▲ JOHN WELSH MEMORIAL FOUNTAIN

"faithful service to his native city and country" by his friends on the site of the Centennial Exhibition of 1876, with which his name is inseparably identified. President of the National Board of Trade from 1866–81, Welsh was also one of the energetic original Fairmount Park commissioners and became the principal officer and president of the Centennial Board of Finance. The giant fountain no longer functions but is intact, and plans call for the Please Touch Museum to restore it.

Next, head for Horticultural Hall on Horticultural Drive in West Fairmount Park, also on the site of Philadelphia's 1876 Centennial celebration grounds. Inside the Center, in the greenhouse, are several fountains.

The **Seaweed Girl Fountain** was created by Philadelphia artist Beatrice Fenton (1887–1983) around 1920. A local businessman approached the Fairmount Park Commission in 1921 with the offer to donate this figure "completely mounted in the pool." The work was accepted that year and installed along Sedgeley Drive in Fairmount Park. Years later, Fenton was asked to add to the work, which she did by creating two groups of angelfish swimming through a coral reef. In 1974, the fish were stolen, and the figure was relocated to its present site. The "Seaweed Girl" was Fenton's first attempt at an ambitious, lifesize, ornamental sculpture. Working in her third-floor studio at 1523 Chestnut Street, she posed a lively, six-year-old child on a box and borrowed a green turtle from the aquarium at the Fairmount Waterworks to serve as a model for the girl's precarious perch. The child is gawky yet charming, posing in her seaweed festoons with all the coy bravado of one caught in the act of dressing up in her mother's clothes before a mirror. The child's toes grip the turtle's back, and her stocky torso balances awkwardly atop thin and knock-kneed legs. This work was awarded The Pennsylvania Academy of the Fine Arts' Widener Gold Medal in 1922, as well as a bronze medal that year at the sesquicentennial. Although it no longer functions as a fountain, it is beautifully displayed among plants and flowers.

The **Centennial Fountain** is a work that Margaret Foley (1827–77) created in 1876. This was her major project of the 1870s and was originally intended for a site in Chicago, but after the great Chicago fire of 1871, the commission was withdrawn. Foley then carved the statue in marble for exhibition in the centennial's horticultural building.

Under an umbrella of sculptured leaves sit lifesize figures of three children. One boy is blowing a horn, another boy puts his foot in to test the water, and

▲ SEAWEED GIRL FOUNTAIN

a girl seems to be deciding whether to try the pool at all. The water spills over the top of the umbrella, which is protecting them from the "rain."

The **Nereid Fountain,** designed by Beatrice Fenton, is no longer a fountain but a wonderful sculpture that plays in between great plantings in the green-house. In the 1950s, when the original Horticultural Hall was damaged by a hurricane and taken down, this fountain went into storage. In 1976, it was rein-stalled in the new Horticultural Center for the nation's bicentennial.

Two more fountains can be found on these grounds. The **Rebecca at the Well Fountain** was designed by John J. Boyle and donated by the Fountain Soci-ety as a bequest of Rebecca Darby Smith in 1908. The fountain would, according to the inscription on it, "ornament the city that William Penn founded . . . refresh the weary and thirsty, both man and beast and . . . com-memorate a fact of Sacred History." The subject is Rebecca offering water to a stranger and his camels (Genesis 24:19). The fountain was originally located at 12th and Spring Garden Streets, but it was moved to the park in 1934. Today it no longer functions as a fountain. The beautiful **Reflecting Pool and Fountains** were built in 1976 for the city's Bicentennial and is on the foot-print of the original Sunken Gardens of the Centennial. It has lovely water-falls and plantings in and alongside the pool.

Next, pay a visit to the **Catholic Total Abstinence Union Fountain,** located on the Centennial grounds on North Concourse Drive and State Street, just east of the Mann Center for the Performing Arts. The fountain was designed by Isaac H. Hobbs and Son and sculpted by German artist Hermann Kirn in about 1876. At the time of its design, it was thought by the Abstinence Union that a fountain of water surrounded by statues of prominent Irish Catholic Revolutionary heroes would be a lasting memorial to the principles of the

▲ REFLECTING POOL AND FOUNTAINS

anti-alcohol organization and of the patriotism of the Irish in America.

The fountain, with figures carved in marble, depicts a 16-ton Moses, who resembles the Moses Acqua Felice Fountain in Rome; John Barry (1745–1803), first commodore of the U.S. Navy; Charles Carroll (1737–1832), a signer of the Declaration of Independence; Archbishop John Carroll (1735–1815), the first Roman Catholic bishop in America; and the Rev. Theobald Matthew (1790–1856), leader of the Abstinence Union. Costing $54,400, the fountain consists of a granite platform in the form of a Maltese cross and

◀ CATHOLIC ABSTINENCE FOUNTAIN

is approached by steps that extend entirely around it. The fountain rises from a mass of rockwork in the center of the basin. At the end of each arm on the cross were drinking fountains surmounted by the 9-foot statues. Moses points toward heaven as the source of water.

At points around the circular wall are medallion decorations. Represented are George Meade, a Revolutionary Philadelphian (grandfather of the Civil War general); Col. Stephen Moylan, a Revolutionary soldier; Count Casimir Pulaski; the Marquis de Lafayette; Comte de Grasse; Chief Orono, Penobscot Indian; and the badge of the Abstinence Union. At the base of each monument, water was dispensed through a lion's mouth.

The fountain currently is not working but is well worth the visit to see it just the same. As of this writing, efforts are under way to raise funds to restore the fountain to working order and back to its former glory.

Another handsome fountain that is no longer working but is still intact and worth a look is the **Orestes and Pylades Fountain,** at Columbia Avenue and 33rd Street in East Fairmount Park, designed by the German artist Carl Johann Steinhauser (1813–1879). The fountain, honoring friendship, shows the two seated figures of Orestes and Pylades with a bust of Diana on a plinth behind them. Pylades was the son of the king of Phocis and grew up with Orestes, who had been exiled to that court to protect him from the vengeance of Clytemnestra and Aegisthus. The friendship between the two young men was as proverbial as that of David and Jonathan. The fountain is a characteristic example of German fondness for placing monuments in public places to serve as daily reminders of virtues and ideals.

The Parkway

In 1884, C. K. Landis, the founder of Vineland, New Jersey, published a drawing showing a wide boulevard from City Hall to the present site of the museum as an entrance to the park. This is precisely the route of the present Benjamin Franklin Parkway.

The best place to start your tour of the Parkway Fountains is at the **Love Park Fountain,** located in the Kennedy Plaza at 15th Street and J. F. Kennedy Boulevard. This world-famous *Love* sculpture was erected in 1976 for the nation's bicentennial celebration. This particular arrangement of the four letters L-O-V-E debuted in a painting by pop artist Robert Indiana in 1964. He then designed the sculpture based on the painting, which was immortalized by the U.S. Post Office on an 8-cent stamp in 1973. The fountain behind the painted aluminum sculpture has a jet spray that sends water sky-high before it descends into a cauldron of roiling water and bounces into a giant pool.

Two blocks west, up the Benjamin Franklin Parkway at 17th Street, the **Tuscan Girl Fountain** stands at the rear of the Embassy Suites Tower. This sculpture and fountain were designed by Oscar Stonorov and Jorio Vivarelli and were dedicated on June 9, 1965. Standing 26 feet high, this bronze marvel was built with funds required by the city's fine-arts ordinance, which earmarks one percent of the city's construction budget for public art.

A few steps away, at 17th and Cherry Streets, is the **Bell Atlantic Plaza Fountain.** This wonderful water display was designed by the Kling-Lindquist Partnership when the Bell Atlantic Tower was built in 1990. During the week, this plaza is filled with employees from the surrounding office buildings taking a lunch break. There are many places to sit around the huge pool, which is always filled with the sounds of water splashing.

Step over to 18th Street at the Parkway and enjoy the lovely and serene **Water Steps Fountain** at the Four Seasons Hotel. In appropriate weather, the hotel serves lunch in the Courtyard Cafe above the

▲ BELL ATLANTIC PLAZA FOUNTAIN

▲ WATER STEPS FOUNTAIN

waterfall. You can also enjoy a series of other fountains on the grounds of the hotel, as well as another interior fountain in the lobby.

When you head outside, before long you will be at the glorious **Swann Memorial Fountain** on Logan Square, which was named for James Logan (1674–1751), William Penn's agent and mayor of Philadelphia. The fountain itself was named for Dr. Wilson Cary Swann. This spectacular fountain was designed by Alexander Stirling Calder (1870–1945). By day, powerful water jets soar 50 feet high into the air to create a magical, liquid architecture. By night, the fountain is illuminated with magnificent, shimmering lighting, an exhilarating sight to see.

Calder called his achievement the Fountain of the Three Rivers. "It was my fancy to imagine the three great decorative bronze figures as the rivers enclosing Philadelphia," he explained. "The Delaware represented by the male

▲ SWANN MEMORIAL FOUNTAIN

Indian, the Schuylkill (or gentle river) south of this, and the Wissahickon (or hidden creek) to the west."

The pool for the fountain—a 124-foot basin, low-curbed, unadorned, and rimmed with Milford pink granite—was finished on November 11, 1920. It took Calder several years to complete the three monumental figures. "When I make a statue for Philadelphia," he said, "I want it to be as big and comprehensive as possible." Calder's father, Alexander Milne Calder (1846–1923), designed and carved the statue of William Penn that sits high above City Hall, as well as 250 other statues in and on City Hall. Calder's son, Alexander "Sandy" Calder (1898–1976), was best known for his mobiles.

The completed fountain was unveiled to the public on July 23, 1924, the eve of the hottest day of the year. According to reports, more than ten thousand sweltering people tangoed in the streets around the fountain to the music of the police band. The unveiling and dedication of such public works were planned to inspire patriotic spirit. The nineteenth-century tradition of pageantry and spectacle often included bunting, music, speeches, fireworks, and even time off from school or work. Dedication ceremonies were memorable events inviting wide public participation.

Continue to stroll down Philadelphia's glorious Benjamin Franklin Parkway, which was inspired by the Champs Élysées in Paris, until you come to the Rodin Museum at 22nd Street. Greeting you outside is the world-famous sculpture of *The Thinker*. Step into the garden in front of the museum building, and you will find a gentle pool and fountain. Inside the museum is the most important collection outside of Paris of works by the celebrated French sculptor Auguste Rodin. Here are housed 127 sculptures in all, in a wonderful building designed by the two great French Neoclassical architects working in Philadelphia at that time: Paul P. Cret and Jacques Greber. The Rodin Museum opened in 1929.

Continue your walk down the Parkway until you come to the Philadelphia Museum of Art. Founded in 1876, it is one of the premier art museums in America. The striking Neoclassical building was constructed in 1928. Inside you will find masterpieces of painting, sculpture, prints, and drawings displayed with a wide range of furniture, silver, and glasswork.

Below the museum stands the colossal **Washington Monument Fountain,** designed by Rudolf Siemering, on Eakins Oval. It is flanked by two large, circular fountains reminiscent of those seen in Rome. According to Penny Balkin Bach's *Public Art of Philadelphia,* the monument is constructed in

▲ WASHINGTON MONUMENT FOUNTAIN

three zones or levels, each representing a different concept: Washington, the hero, sits at the top; allegorical figures depicting his time are on the middle level; and on the lowest level are the flora and fauna of his country, with representative human figures. On this extraordinary Washington Monument, a large bison meditates on the perpetual traffic jam amid jets, pools, and competing fauna.

This project was a long time in the planning and the making. Siemering was given a contract in 1880 and promised, in his words, "a monument so

◀ WASHINGTON MONUMENT FOUNTAIN

grand, as there has never been one executed to my knowledge." He had deliberately not considered the costs but had composed freely. As sponsors of the undertaking, the Society of the Cincinnati could not afford to be so cavalier in their handling of the finances, and it was fortunate for their purposes that on June 19, 1880, the trusteeship of the Washington Monument Fund was handed over to them from the Pennsylvania Company. This put an additional $55,676 at their disposal, which enabled them to authorize Siemering to proceed with his ambitious schemes. It took Siemering a staggering sixteen years to model and cast the Washington Monument, but it had taken the Society of the Cincinnati almost seventy years to raise the necessary funds.

So it was that after years of delay and setbacks, President William McKinley finally unveiled the monument in a long-awaited ceremony on May 5, 1897. The day was declared a public holiday, and all kinds of celebrations took place. The unveiling was thus a national event and recognized on a national scale the single-mindedness of the Society of the Cincinnati of Pennsylvania in achieving its goal.

In 1928, when the Benjamin Franklin Parkway became a reality, the Washington Monument was moved from its rather remote original site at

▼ WASHINGTON MONUMENT FOUNTAIN

the Green Street entrance of Fairmount Park to the prominent location it now occupies.

Before leaving the front of the Art Museum, climb the steps to see the Henry M. Phillips Memorial Fountain. Called **Courtship,** it sits at the top of the steps in the East Court and was designed by Henry Mitchell (1915–80). The fountain contains eight bronze bas-reliefs 30 inches in height. It was commissioned by the commissioners of Fairmount Park and the Philadelphia Museum of Art and was installed in 1958. The water jets shoot a glorious cascade of water high into the air.

Cross back over the Parkway at 24th Street, where you will see the beautiful gilded bronze statue of *Joan of Arc,* a work created by the French artist Emmanuel Fremiet. In 1889, the French community in Philadelphia, with the aid of the Fairmount Park Art Association, purchased a statue of Joan from

▼ COURTSHIP FOUNTAIN

▲ PHILADELPHIAN FOUNTAIN WORKS

Fremiet, with the stipulation that there would only be three editions of the work: one in Paris, one in Philadelphia, and a third in Nancy, France. The statue was unveiled on November 15, 1890, with extensive fanfare. In 1960, the Art Association gilded Joan and placed her near the Art Museum. Natives refer to her as Joanie on a Pony. You will pass this landmark on your way to the entrance of the high-rise condo building the Philadelphian, in front of which is the **Philadelphian Fountain Works.** A wide display of multiple jets provides dancing waters that crisscross one another in an aquatic ballet.

Rittenhouse Square Area

THE TOUR OF THE RITTENHOUSE SQUARE AREA FOUNTAINS BEGINS AT FITLER Square, located at 23rd and Pine Streets, at the district's southwestern edge. The square was named in 1896 in honor of Edwin H. Fitler (1825–96), mayor of Philadelphia from 1887 to 1891. The wonderful Victorian **Fitler Square Fountain** sits in the middle of this lovely neighborhood park, surrounded by attractive and playful sculptures. Take time to enjoy exploring this special space, which is still very much a nineteenth-century Philadelphia park. You can rest on one of the many benches before heading through mostly nineteenth-century residential streets (don't miss the serene and handsome blocks of Delancey Street between 21st and 19th Streets) to historic Rittenhouse Square itself, which is bounded by Walnut and Locust Streets and 18th and 19th Streets.

Rittenhouse Square, anchoring one of the most harmonious urban neighborhoods in America, is also the most beloved of the five city squares laid out by William Penn and Surveyor General Thomas Holme. It originally served as a pasture for stray cows, pigs, and chickens. Then the neighborhood's mid-nineteenth-century gentrification graced it with great Victorian mansions. Now stately apartment buildings frame the square, which boasts a children's wading pool and fountain, wooden benches, overarching trees, and fine statuary. Much of the park's intimate ambience is due to Paul Phillippe Cret, whose designs for the wading pool, central plaza, and entrances, reminiscent

of European parks with fountains and statuary, were completed in 1913. Originally called Southwest Square, the square was named after the great eighteenth-century Philadelphia astronomer and mathematician, David Rittenhouse, in 1913. In the beautiful pool near the square's center is a bronze statue of **Duck Girl,** by Paul Manship (1885–1917). This charming young girl in Greek costume was exhibited in 1914 at the Pennsylvania Academy of the Fine Arts, where it won the Widener Gold Medal. The Committee on the Works of Art of the Fairmount Park Association decided to purchase *Duck Girl* from the exhibition. Originally placed in Cloverly

▲ WELCOME FOUNTAIN

Park at Wissahickon Street and School Lane, *Duck Girl* was damaged and was removed to storage in 1956. From there, she was rescued by the Rittenhouse Square Improvement Association.

On the west side of the square sits the elegant and gracious Rittenhouse Hotel, which often hosts visiting dignitaries and film stars. In the courtyard of this hotel is the **Welcome Fountain,** with a sculptured woman in the center with arms outstretched in a welcoming gesture as she stands surrounded by spouting fountains.

From inside the lobby, you will enter the Rittenhouse's beautiful garden, where tea and lunch are served. In this lovely garden is the **Rittenhouse Hotel Garden Fountain.** You'll hear the soothing sounds of falling water into a basin from three fountain heads.

Right across the street from the Sheraton Hotel, on the east side of the square, is the world-famous Curtis Institute of Music, one of the finest music schools in the world. A half block away, on 18th Street, is the Philadelphia Art Alliance, America's oldest multidisciplinary arts center, housed in a beautiful, turn-of-the-century Italianate building, which was home to the founder, Christine Wetherill.

▲ CHESTNUT PARK FOUNTAINS

▲ COMMERCE SQUARE FOUNTAIN

Stroll to 17th Street and head north to Chestnut Street. Just off the north-east corner of 17th and Chestnut lies a tiny oasis called **Chestnut Park,** a charming pocket park. Lots of greenery and benches surround a cluster of concrete towers, with water falling over different heights into a delightful splashing pool; this is a unique sculptural achievement.

Next, head back to 19th Street, and go north one block to Market Street to the Philadelphia Stock Exchange. When you enter the lobby, you will feel that you are in the Hanging Gardens of Babylon. A spectacular haven of greenery awaits you with creatively designed fountains throughout this block-long oasis. It is delightful to descend the steps into this fertile green space, with the sights and sounds of falling water all around you.

In the lobby of the office building at 2000 Market Street, you will find a beautiful, black ebony fountain, with water cascading over its four-tier-high wall. One block away is **Commerce Square,** between 21st and 22nd Streets. In the outdoor courtyard is a large, spectacular fountain with dancing waters. Tables and chairs surround the fountain if you want to stop and enjoy the scenery.

The Historic District

THE TOUR OF THE HISTORIC DISTRICT FOUNTAINS STARTS AT 4TH AND
Locust Streets, on the southwest corner. Here you will find the Episcopal
Diocese of Pennsylvania Church House, in a handsome Georgian mansion.
A few paces west on Locust—a block straight out of the eighteenth century,
filled with residences that today serve as homes for National Historic Park
employees—you'll see a tranquil little garden with a small fountain in its
center, surrounded by seasonal flowers.

Stroll a little farther down Locust Street until you come to the **Magnolia
Garden,** and enter through its iron gates. Straight ahead is a wall fountain;
the inscription says it was contributed by the Garden Club of America in
1959 in honor of the founders of our nation. The club also provided funds
for the garden, which is now maintained by the National Park Service.

The garden is a pleasant spot to sit and meditate. The Magnolia Garden was
originally planned as a gathering place for representatives from each of the
then-forty-eight states. A plaque in the garden says that George Washington,
who lived in Philadelphia during his presidency, retained a lively interest in
horticulture. His letters reveal that magnolias were among the trees he hoped
to grow. Although the magnolias in this garden are different from those men-

tioned by Washington, he would have enjoyed their delicate pink flowers in the spring. At the far end of the garden is a pool raining down quiet splashes of water into its basin.

Continue your stroll down Locust Street, and cross to little Randolph Street, where you will find the rear garden of the Athenaeum of Philadelphia, a special-collections library and historic site museum founded in 1814. The Victorian garden contains a lovely cast-iron, three-tiered fountain.

Turn back to Locust Walk, and cross 6th Street into **Washington Square.** This was one of the four original squares in William Penn's grand design to create a "greene Country Towne." Under the spreading canopy of sycamores, locusts, basswoods, and ginkgos lie the remains of Continental soldiers and British prisoners, casualties of deeds done in transforming Penn's holy experiment into one of self-government.

In the middle of the square, you'll find another large, circular fountain with a central spray of water in the middle; the water jet changes heights during the day. Benches surround the fountain, if you want to take a break. This fountain was recently renovated, thanks to a grant from the Philadelphia Fountain Society and the film company Declaration Productions, which filmed the Nicolas Cage movie *National Treasure* here in the square and elsewhere in Philadelphia. (The Philadelphia Fountain Society has long been dormant, but there has been a corpus of funds kept, and according to a spokesman, the Philadelphia Fountain Society will continue with small projects.)

Before you leave the square, visit the Tomb of the Unknown Soldier and the Eternal Flame, with a wonderful sculpture of George Washington. In front of Washington is a tomb that reads, "Beneath This Stone Rests a Soldier of Washington's Army Who Died to Give You Liberty." This is the only tomb in the United States built in memory of unknown Revolutionary soldiers.

When you leave Washington Square, head to the south side, to a thirty-three-story condominium building called **Hopkinson House,** built in 1962 and designed by architect Oscar Stonorov (1905–70). It was the first high-rise residential building in Society Hill and was named for Francis Hopkinson, a lawyer, composer, signer of the Declaration of Independence, and designer of the American flag. Ask at the front desk if you can visit the garden and fountains in the rear of the lobby. In 1996, the Hopkinson House restoration project installed an attractive double waterfall and pool in the south plaza of the building. It covered a blank concrete retaining wall and used a portion of the original but nonfunctioning circulating water moat that surrounds the plaza. The balance of the moat was converted into a flowerbed. The design of the pool and the recirculating water system was done by Schwam Architects in 1996. The shadow-sunlight tile pattern was a collab-

▼ WASHINGTON SQUARE FOUNTAIN

▲ HOPKINSON HOUSE GARDEN FOUNTAIN

oration of the Schwam group and Edwin P. Rothong, the Hopkinson House engineering advocate. Take time to walk around this lovely garden. Near the waterfall is a bronze sculpture, *Adam and Eve*, by Lucius Crowell.

Walk back through Washington Square to the Curtis Publishing Company building at the corner of 6th Street and Walnut Street. The building was the original home of such publications as *Saturday Evening Post, Ladies Home Journal, Holiday,* and *Jack & Jill Magazine.* In the 6th Street lobby of this gorgeous building, you will discover a magnificent wall mural and pool fountain, the **Dream Garden.** Beautiful mountains and shimmering waterfalls adorn this monumental mosaic. Created by Maxfield Parrish and Louis Comfort Tiffany, it is a breathtaking 15-by-49-foot work made entirely of shimmering glass. An inspiring example of creative collaboration and artistic innovation on a grand scale, it is one of only three such works of its kind ever undertaken by the famed Tiffany Studio, under the direction of Louis Comfort Tiffany. Publishers Cyrus Curtis and Edward Bok believed that art belonged in public buildings where many people could enjoy it, and they chose this sweeping wall space as the place for the crowning touch to the Curtis Publishing Company's magnificent new headquarters.

The Dream Garden originated as an oil painting commissioned of famed Philadelphia-born artist Maxfield Parrish, whose meticulous fantasies had long impressed Bok. In 1914, Tiffany began the work of translating Parrish's vision of a world without time, trouble, and tension into luminous beauty.

▲ DREAM GARDEN FOUNTAIN

▲ CURTIS CENTER COURT FOUNTAIN

This glorious work took more than one hundred thousand pieces of glass in 260 color tones to make. Most of the glass was set in twenty-four panels in Tiffany's New York Studios. Installing the panels took six months. The finished work, the second-largest Tiffany mosaic in the world, was hailed by critics as "a veritable wonderpiece" at the official unveiling in 1916. The amazing variety of opaque, translucent, and transparent glass, entirely lighted from the lobby, achieves perspective effects that have never been duplicated. The work sits behind a quiet pool of water, with two low base fountains.

Walk past the Tiffany mural to the other side of the building lobby and into the soaring, twelve-story-high Fountain Court, with its witty neo-Egyptian design; potted palms are placed atop high columns to lead your eye up to the glass-topped roof. At ground level, the wonderful, majestic **Court Fountain** flows over tiers of travertine green and black and white marble.

▲ MILKWEED POD FOUNTAIN

▲ VOYAGE OF ULYSSES FOUNTAIN

Retrace your steps back to 6th Street and head north one block toward Market Street; you'll pass the Rohm and Haas Chemical Company building. Walk up a few steps and through the courtyard. In front of you will be the **Milkweed Pod Fountain,** a copper and stainless steel sculpture. Designed by Clark B. Fitzgerald, it was dedicated in 1965. Rohm and Haas commissioned Fitzgerald to design the fountain for the courtyard in their new headquarters on Independence Mall, under the aegis of the Redevelopment Authority's Fine Arts Program. The sculpture combines a natural image, the release of milkweed seeds into a breeze, with formal geometric elements. Bright stainless steel seeds contrast with the weathered green copper pod.

To complete your Historic District tour of fountains, head north again on 6th Street, crossing Market Street. You will pass the James A. Byrne Federal

Courthouse and the William J. Green Jr. Federal Building. Between them, in the plaza, is the dramatic **Voyage of Ulysses Fountain.**

This is another stainless steel structure, but in a giant watery base. This magical work was designed by artist David von Schlegell. Commissioned as part of the Art-in-Architecture Program of the General Services Administration, the work was dedicated in 1976. As students of mythology know, Ulysses wandered for a decade on the Mediterranean Sea before reaching his homeland. Von Schlegell's design features diagonal lines to counter the verticality of the architecture. Peggy Balkin Bach describes the fountain: "In basic shape, *Voyage of Ulysses* resembles a sail, but its appearance varies from the viewer's different perspectives. Hydraulic engineers assisted von Schlegell in producing dramatic effects with the water as it scampers against and through the sculpture." The visit to this fountain brings the Historic District fountain tour to a dramatic close.

One more optional stop is a historic park, with a giant circular fountain that is in disrepair and out of commission. Continue up 6th Street and cross Race Street to Franklin Square, one of the original green parks envisioned for Philadelphia by William Penn when he laid out the city in 1682. Originally called Northeast Square, it was renamed for Benjamin Franklin in 1825. The fountain sits in the middle of the square. As of this writing, the Fairmount Park Commission is repairing the fountain and restoring the park.

Penn's Landing

PENN'S LANDING, A TRACT OF WATERFRONT LAND EXTENDING FROM SOUTH
Street north to Vine Street, has been developed into one of the city's most
important recreational sites.

In 1967, with most of the shipping concentrated at the south end of
Philadelphia, rotting piers were replaced with a system of walkways and a
tiered river-view amphitheater known as the Great Plaza. Pedestrian walkways at Market, Chestnut, Walnut, and South Streets cross Interstate 95 to
connect the city with the waterfront.

Once the city's primary commercial area, this is where William Penn's surveyor, Thomas Holmes, started parceling out land grants beginning in the
1680s. By 1700, most Philadelphians lived three or four blocks from the river
on tiny, congested lots—a far cry from Penn's dream of a "greene Country
Towne." Through the eighteenth and nineteenth centuries, and well into the
twentieth, the docks were central to city commerce.

In the early 1800s, America was entering an exciting period of rapid development. The success of American trade and the prominence of Philadelphia
as a port for seagoing traffic fed local artists' love of ships and gave countless
opportunities for sketching river views. In the early 1820s and 1830s, the pop-
ulation of the nation, particularly in the cities, grew dramatically as a result

◀ GREAT PLAZA FOUNTAIN

of large-scale immigration. Innovations in transportation and communication began to alter the face of the American landscape and to enlarge the nation's vision. Railroads and canals, improved postal service, and the telegraph linked people together and accelerated the pace of American life and cultural development. Along with prosperity and optimism came a strong push for self-identification, which was manifested in nationalistic movements and publications. In the arts, the production of seascapes and landscapes with reassuring messages about expansion and about America's destiny helped alleviate some of the uncertainty caused by the rapid change.

The tour of the fountains at Penn's Landing starts with the **Great Plaza Fountains.** Head for Market Street at Columbus Boulevard, where you will discover a wide expanse of public space surrounded with numerous fountains of cascading waters.

When you have finished admiring these playful fountains, stroll along the river's edge and walk up to the International Sculpture Garden, located at Columbus Boulevard (sometimes called Delaware Avenue) between Chestnut Street and Spruce Street, alongside the Hyatt Hotel. The International Sculpture Garden was dedicated in celebration of the nation's bicentennial in 1976.

GREAT PLAZA FOUNTAIN ▼

▲ FIVE WATER SPOUTS, FROG, AND LINTEL

Conceived by the Fairmount Park Art Association in the 1960s, the idea was to celebrate the influences of other cultures in the American experience.

Here you find several fountains, including **Five Water Spouts, Frog, and Lintel.** These sculptures date from the twelfth and thirteenth centuries. Made of volcanic stone, the works come from Java, Indonesia, and were not installed until 1986. In the first decades of the eighth century, religious monuments dedicated to Hindu deities and Buddhist thought were built on the islands of Java and Sumatra in Indonesia. These temples were sanctuaries to gods and often seen as monuments to the kings, believed to be the living spirits of the gods. Their shapes were based on Indian temple forms and were thought to represent Mount Meru (Mountain of the Gods), symbolizing the return of the souls of the deceased royalty to the realm of the gods. Elaborate relief carvings, now worn with time, decorated the walls with rich imagery that related to the individuals' achievements in life, previous incarnations, and religious and moral teachings.

The sites of the temples in eastern Java often had pools for ritual bathing. Carved spouts such as those seen here would channel the heavy water flow. From left to right, the more familiar tiger, ram, elephant, and frog sitting in the pool basin are in the company of two *makaras*, mythical creatures that appear throughout Indian and Indonesian art. The overhead lintel depicts a *kala*, another fantastic creature thought to be a ferocious but protective force. According to tradition, the *kala*, placed above a doorway, intiated a cycle of rebirth for the visitor who passed through the gate. The visitor, who was symbolically devoured and immediately reborn, thus experienced the endless cycle of rebirth of all living things.

In the same vicinity is the giant **Sphere Fountain.** This pre-Columbian granite monolith, weighing almost 24,000 pounds, is from a site near Palmar Sur in the delta of Costa Rica's Disquis River. Large spheres like this were placed on platforms or grouped in patterns or lines of as many as fifteen spheres, possibly astronomical alignments. Local people still value them highly without knowing the religious or magical purposes for which they were originally

▼ SPHERE FOUNTAIN

▲ UNA BIFORCAZIONE E TRE PAESAGGI

made. This piece was obtained by the Fairmount Park Art Association with the cooperation of the Costa Rican government and the United Fruit Company in 1969, and was installed in 1976.

Continuing the tour, walk to 2nd Street and Walnut Street, to the Society Hill Sheraton Hotel. In the lobby, you will find a large sculptural fountain by Giuseppe Penone called **Una Biforcazione e Tre Paesaggi,** meaning A Forked Branch and Three Landscapes. This work was commissioned by Rouse and Associates as part of the Redevelopment Authority's Fine Arts Program. The artist is associated with an Italian movement known as "poor art." The artists of this movement use commonplace materials to express history, culture, mythology, and the relationship between human beings and the environment.

In Penone's design, water bubbles quietly through the larger end of a long, bronze branch in the circular fountain. Large clay pots contain low plants,

▼ SOCIETY HILL TOWERS PLAZA FOUNTAIN

vines, and bushes. Three figures have a barklike coating: One is sitting with her feet in the water; one is reclining near the edge of the fountain; and the third seems to be stepping away from the pool.

When you leave the Sheraton, walk to nearby 3rd Street and Walnut Street. On the corner is the garden next to the Bishop White House, with stately willow oaks, holly, and boxwood hedges. This garden was originally the site of the home of Dr. Benjamin Rush, a signer of the Declaration of Independence. The garden has a charming wall fountain with tumbling waters. You can spend some time relaxing on a bench in this cool garden.

Next, head back south to 2nd Street and Locust Street, where you'll find the **Society Hill Towers,** a trio of high-rise condo buildings designed by I. M. Pei, of Pei Cobb Freed and Partners. In the courtyard, you'll find a wonderful fountain surrounded by beautiful landscaping all year round. The courtyard also contains a trio of sculptures by artist Leonard Baskin, called *Old Man, Young Man,* and *The Future.* A young man, standing, and an older man, seated, confront a winged creature representing the future.

End your Penn's Landing tour by going to **Head House Square** at 2nd Street and Lombard Street, where you will find a fountain playfully splashing in a cobblestone base with three tiers of steps to sit on. Sometimes the city gets playful by adding color to the water.

Market Street East

THE TOUR OF THE MARKET STREET EAST FOUNTAINS BEGINS ON THE NORTH-
east corner of 10th Street and Locust Street, at the Bluemle Life Sciences
Building. Built in 1991 by Jefferson University, this is one of the nation's fore-
most medical centers. Outside its plaza is the **Water Falls Fountain,** a wonderful water creation. Water from above spills over two dozen slabs of narrow
ledges, ending up in the pool below. It is a marvelous fountain that brings
delight to all who see it.

Walk over to 9th Street and Chestnut Street. Inside the **Benjamin Franklin
House,** an apartment and office building on Chestnut Street, you'll find the
delightful, quiet lobby fountain. From a beautiful Grecian urn in a bronze
pool, water dances up into the air, whirling as its falls.

Now head up one block to Market Street at 9th Street, and enter the **Gallery**
shopping mall. More than forty thousand people pass through this bustling
space every day. On the lower level, right in front of the glass-enclosed eleva-
tors, sits a pool of dancing waters and lights. It's a refreshing place to stop for
a break, if you're so inclined. You can also take the elevator up to view the
fountain from above.

◀ WATER FALLS FOUNTAIN

▲ BEN FRANKLIN HOUSE LOBBY FOUNTAIN

▲ GALLERY FOUNTAIN

A short distance away, in the Strawbridge's department store at the center of the first floor, is *Il Porcellino,* a bronze statue of a wild boar. Rising 31 inches in height, the boar sits on a black marble base in a pool with water dripping from the animal's mouth. Many people like to toss a coin and make a wish. This is the fifth known cast of the wild boar in the Straw Market in Florence, Italy. The cast was commissioned by Ferdinando Martinelli of Florence and was rented by Strawbridge's for an Italian festival and subsequently bought in 1966.

The next stop is at 11th Street and Walnut Street, back on the Jefferson University campus, where you'll find the **Fountain of Sea Lions.** Five young sea lions play in the falling water, with one holding court on top of the rock in the pool's center. Sitting on a nearby bench and watching this delightful fountain for a few minutes will leave you feeling refreshed.

Continue up 11th Street to the Aramark Building at Market Street. Inside the lobby, you will find the **Day Dream Fountain.** Here, two black bronze reclining female figures by sculptor Ronald Bateman sit by a pool's edge and a lighted-from-behind waterfall, which flows down into a pond surrounded with plantings. A three-paneled mural of artistic variations on Fairmount

▼ FOUNTAIN OF SEA LIONS

▲ DAY DREAM FOUNTAIN

▲ MARRIOTT HOTEL LOBBY FOUNTAIN

▲ BELLEVUE PARK HYATT HOTEL FOUNTAIN

▲ CITY HALL FOUNTAIN

▲ CITY HALL CASCADING FOUNTAIN

Park by artist Walter Erlebacher decorates the wall behind the fountain. This project was developed by One Reading Center Associates in cooperation with the Redevelopment Authority, the City of Philadelphia, and the Commonwealth of Pennsylvania, and was dedicated in 1985.

Next, head down Market Street to the **Marriott Hotel** at 12th Street and enter the lobby. Rising in front of you is a very twenty-first-century fountain. What looks like part of a miniature gold spaceship, with steam emanating from its top, stands in an odd-shaped pool with the water falling into oblivion on each side. You can sit alongside this fountain and relax with a cool drink from the bar, if you so desire.

Walk over to **Bellevue Park Hyatt Hotel** at Broad Street and Walnut Street, to see two more fountains. The old and revered Bellevue Stratford still stands but is now under new management. Take the escalator down to the lower level, which is a food court. There, by the escalator, you will find a statue of *Diana* standing in a pool with upward sprinklings of water. Then take the elevator, located in the hotel lobby in the rear of the building, to the twelfth-floor conservatory. In the court of the conservatory, which is frequently used for food service and private parties, you will find a wonderful three-tiered bronze Victorian fountain.

For your last stop on this tour, head back north on Broad Street to City Hall. On the 15th Street side is the wonderful contemporary **City Hall Fountain.** Staying on the same plaza, look for the **Cascading Fountain** on the level below. Then take the nearby stairs down to view the fountain waterfall in all its splendor. You can also go behind the falls to view it from inside the cascade.

Other Fountains in the Philadelphia Area

THE UNIVERSITY MUSEUM FOUNTAINS

Founded in 1887, the University Museum of the University of Pennsylvania, at 34th Street and Spruce Street on the Penn campus, has been an international leader in archaeological research, sponsoring more than four hundred expeditions to all parts of the inhabited world. The museum has several fountains worth visiting.

In the lower courtyard of the main entrance is the handsome **Wall Fountain** designed by Alexander S. Calder (1870–1945), whose son achieved fame as the inventor of mobile sculpture. Built in 1929, the fountain is sculpted with birds and a mask. Opposite the wall fountain, in the center of the courtyard, is a large circular pool, also built in 1929. Originally two Pompeian reproduction figures sat in the pool, but when the courtyard was restored in 2002, a marble bowl and sphere, designed by the Olin Partnership, were added.

In the **Upper Courtyard,** you will find a large pool with a fountain, designed in 1896. Walter Cope, one of the associated architects of the museum project, wrote to a trustee that the principal entrance to the first part of the building would be erected "through a park or botanic garden, which will contain

▲ UNIVERSITY MUSEUM UPPER COURTYARD FOUNTAIN

▲ DOLPHIN FOUNTAIN

a large pool or basin especially designed to become a lily or water garden." The garden was to be designed in the style of the gardens of Italian and Spanish villas. In 2003, the museum began a major renovation of the upper courtyard, now called the Stoner Courtyard, which includes restoring the pool and fountain, modeled on the original plans. This work is scheduled to be completed by the end of summer 2004. Do make a visit here.

The **Dolphin Fountain,** in North Philadelphia at 10th Street and Jefferson Street, is located in the large Schwartz playground. The modern sculpture in the middle of the fountain, designed by Joseph C. Bailey, contains a jet spraying water over three fiberglass dolphins playing below. Funds were provided through the Redevelopment Authority's one percent Fine Arts Program, and the fountain was installed in 1972.

Ascension Manor, a residential complex at 8th and Poplar Streets, has a fountain in its courtyard. Designed by Christopher Ray, the wrought copper fountain is 84 inches high and its basin is 180 inches in diameter. Installed in 1970, this is another water sculpture built with funds provided through the Redevelopment Authority's one percent Fine Arts Program.

THE MORRIS ARBORETUM

The Morris Arboretum of the University of Pennsylvania is located at 100 Northwestern Avenue in Chestnut Hill. Its 92 public acres are set in a romantic landscape garden of winding paths, streams, and special garden areas. Visitors discover hidden grottoes, a number of fountains, and Japanese rockwork. The Morris Arboretum began in 1887 as Compton, the home of John and Lydia Morris.

The **Water Staircase Fountain,** located in the English Park section of the arboretum, was commissioned in 1916 by Lydia Morris in memory of her brother, John, who had died shortly before. The fountain faced the mansion, which no longer exists, and would have been easily viewed from its windows. After decades of deterioration, the fountain was restored and a new sculpture, *After B. K. S. Iyenger,* was installed in 1988.

The **Sylk Fountain,** at the Pennock Flower Walk, features an original fountain that was purchased by John Morris in 1901. The Flower Walk is a relatively new feature to the arboretum, designed as a tribute to Philadelphia horticulturist Liddon J. Pennock, whose own home and gardens, Meadow-

▲ WATER STAIRCASE FOUNTAIN

▲ ROSE GARDEN FOUNTAIN

▲ MERCURY LOGGIA FOUNTAINS

brook Farm (at 1633 Washington Lane in Meadowbrook, Pennsylvania), are open to the public.

The focal point of the arboretum's famous **Rose Garden** is its fountain, which was installed with a private gift as part of a restoration project in the early 1970s.

The **Mercury Loggia** was constructed in 1913 by John Morris to celebrate the twenty-fifth anniversary of the founding of Compton, his family's summer home. The loggia is a classic stone pavilion that houses the sculpture *Mercury at Rest,* a cast of an original that the Morrises purchased on one of their trips to Italy. The fountains that flank the loggia had not functioned since the mid-1930s, but were restored in 2002.

THE JAMES A. MICHENER ART MUSEUM

The James A. Michener Art Museum, located at 138 South Pine Street in Doylestown, is named for the town's most famous son, the Pulitzer Prize winner and supporter of the arts. The museum opened in 1988 in what had long served as the Bucks County Jail.

▲ WOMAN WASHING HER HAIR FOUNTAIN

▲ HEADWATERS FOUNTAIN

Today the former prison walls enclose the museum's lush backyard, which provides an outdoor gallery. This is the Patricia D. Pfundt Sculpture Garden, in a wonderful natural setting that includes several fountains. One of these is a reflecting pool with a sculpture called **Woman Washing Her Hair,** created in 1954 by Jo Jenks (1903–95). The sculpture sits on a black granite base, with water spilling down in perfect formation. Also in the garden is the **Headwaters Fountain,** which consists of several spurts of water rising at different levels and falling over a circular cobblestone bed.

Doylestown is the Bucks County seat and is well worth the trip. It is a vibrant, small town with much in the way of cultural activities.

Longwood Gardens

KENNETT SQUARE, PENNSYLVANIA

JUST 30 MILES WEST OF PHILADELPHIA, IN KENNETT SQUARE, PENNSYLVANIA, is Longwood Gardens, touted by some as the world's premier horticultural display garden. Longwood now encompasses 1,050 acres of outdoor gardens, twenty indoor gardens with 4 acres of greenhouses, eleven thousand different types of plants, and many spectacular illuminated fountains. Open every day of the year, Longwood boasts more than nine hundred thousand visitors annually and was recently named a "national wonder" by *National Geographic Traveler* magazine.

The gardens were the country home of Pierre S. du Pont (1870–1954), industrial wizard and financier. Pierre was the great-grandson of Eleuthère Irénée du Pont (1771–1834), who arrived in the United States from France in 1800 and founded the DuPont Chemical Company. Pierre turned it into a corporate empire and used his resulting personal fortune to develop and endow his Longwood property.

Pierre du Pont's purchase of the property was the result of years of preparation and travels to Europe, which nurtured his interest in gardens, trees, flowers, and especially fountains. His early years were influenced by the local Brandywine Valley's natural beauty.

◀ MAIN FOUNTAIN GARDENS

In 1886, he had entered MIT near Boston, and the highlight of his college years was a three-month trip in the summer of 1889 to Europe, where he visited the Paris World's Fair and Versailles.

Following graduation in 1890, he secured employment with the DuPont Company in Wilmington. His mother chose this occasion to build a new house for the family, and Pierre was overseer for the project, which included laying out the garden. Du Pont was twenty-three when he visited the 1893 World Columbian Exposition in Chicago. He was impressed by the grandiose effects and later recalled that the fountains there were his inspiration for illuminated water at Longwood.

In 1907, he laid out Longwood's first true flower garden. He filled the 600-foot-long Flower Garden Walk with favorite perennials, biennials, and some annuals. A pool 20 feet in diameter was constructed at the intersection of the main paths. Its simple jet was Longwood's first fountain.

▼ MAIN FOUNTAIN GARDENS

▲ OPEN AIR THEATER FOUNTAINS

In 1910 and 1913, du Pont and his future wife, Alice Belin, visited Italy. The Villa d'Este, outside Rome, was famous for its fountains. On the second trip, they visited twenty-three villas and gardens, including Villa Gori in Sienna, whose outdoor theater provided the inspiration for one at Longwood. The debut of du Pont's theater was at a garden party in 1914 and was a great success with guests. Shortly thereafter, he began experimenting with fountains for the theater stage, which first gushed at the 1915 garden party. Du Pont had built a conservatory in front of rolling countryside; he transformed this site into the formal groundwork for Longwood's **Main Fountain Garden.**

In the mid-1920s, du Pont devoted less time to corporate matters so that he could spend more time on philanthropic and personal interests. The summer of 1925 was capped by a trip to France and a two-week tour of chateaux and gardens. It was at this time that du Pont started the creation of his Italian Water Garden. His inspiration was not the French gardens, but the Villa Gamberaia, near Florence, Italy, which he had visited in 1913.

The Italian original has only a few fountains, but in Longwood's version, more than six hundred jets in nine separate displays shoot from six blue-tiled

▲ ITALIAN GARDEN FOUNTAIN

pools and twelve pedestal basins along the sides. A maximum-capacity 4,500 gallons per minute are recirculated, with the tallest jet in the far pool reaching 40 feet high. A surprise feature is a curving water staircase to the southwest, which complements a traditional staircase to the southeast. The arched wall that connects them and supports the observation terrace is embellished with sculptured fountains and terra cotta jars.

Meanwhile, at the **Open-Air Theater,** a new, much enlarged fountain system was installed, with seven circular basins with removable covers built into the main stage floor. A unique six-foot-high water curtain, two upper-level basins, and isolated roof fountains off to either side complete the water features. Under the stage are eleven pumps recirculating 2,000 gallons of water per minute through 750 nozzles. These are illuminated from below by more than 600 multicolored lights. The jets and lights were originally controlled from a hand-operated switchboard in the spotlight tower behind the audience. Nothing like this had ever been seen before.

According to Colvin Randell in his book on Longwood Gardens, Du Pont was inspired by the success of the Italian Water Garden and the theater to create the ultimate fountain display to rival those he had witnessed at the Chicago fair thirty-five years before. In 1928, to the area south of the conservatory, he added two long canals and two circular pools in the area bounded by the maple trees, and a huge rectangular basin on the far hill. The pools and basins were filled with 380 fountainheads, scuppers, and spouts. A recirculation system of eighteen pumps propels as much as 10,000 gallons of water a minute as high as 130 feet.

The main fountains were first turned on in 1931 and remain spectacular by day. At night, they take on a different look, with 724 lighting units with colored glass filters tinting the water green, blue, red, yellow, and white.

From the point of view of garden history, the Main Fountain Garden is an eclectic assemblage of Italianate ornamentation and French grandeur, with a heavy dose of spectacular showmanship. Its theatricality is dazzling.

The completion of the fountains in the mid-1930s marked an end to major construction during Pierre du Pont's lifetime.

Today spectacular fireworks and fountain displays attract as many as five thousand spectators on summer evenings, and nearly two hundred thousand visitors come to see four thousand lights outdoors at Christmastime.

The 1925 **Italian Water Garden** was completely rebuilt between 1990 and 1992 at a cost of more than $4 million. Much of Longwood's public appeal is due to Pierre du Pont's innate sense of the garden as theater, and this ties Longwood directly to the great gardens of Italy and France and to the spectacular nineteenth-century world's fairs that proclaimed the triumph of technology. Longwood combines gardening arts with technology, and the results are not just remarkable—they're unforgettable! For information, tour reservations, and directions, call Longwood Gardens at 610-388-1000.

Nemours Mansion and Gardens

WILMINGTON, DELAWARE

A TRIP TO THE NEMOURS MANSION, GARDENS, AND FOUNTAINS IS HIGHLY recommended. The estate is, in a word, spectacular. Nemours, the home of Alfred I. du Pont, lies just outside of Wilmington, Delaware. Its name derives from the town in France that du Pont's great-great grandfather, Pierre-Samuel du Pont de Nemours, represented as a member of the French estates general in 1789.

Du Pont de Nemours and his family emigrated to the United States in the aftermath of the French Revolution and settled in the area known as the Brandywine Valley. The Nemours estate today stands on 300 acres.

The mansion was built in 1909–10 by James Smyth and Son of Brandywine granite, all of which was quarried on the estate, and trimmed in Indiana limestone. It was designed by the New York architectural firm of Carere and Hastings, who based the plan loosely on the Petit Trianon, a house at Versailles built by Louis XV for Madame de Pompadour. Du Pont added his own ideas, however, including the recessed portico and the broad front veranda, and the classic French symmetry of the original architect's vision evolved into what one sees today.

◀ SUNKEN GARDENS FOUNTAINS

Du Pont died in 1935, and his wife, Jessie Ball du Pont, continued to occupy the house until her death in 1970. It had been the express wish of the du Ponts that the mansion and gardens be opened for the enjoyment of the public. Soon after Mrs. du Pont's affairs were settled, plans to realize that wish began in earnest.

The estate had always been beautifully maintained, and from the time it opened to the public in 1977, visitors have seen the estate at its best. The mansion, gardens, and fountains have been maintained in their historic splendor. The 47,000-square-foot mansion has 36 rooms open to the public with fine examples of antique furniture, rare rugs, tapestries, and outstanding works of art. It is a home, not a museum, and is furnished to reflect the way it was when the du Ponts lived there. Tour groups are kept small and include commentary by expert guides.

The rooms along the front of the house, which faces northwest, all share a stunning view of the formal gardens. Extending from the mansion to the

▼ REFLECTING POOL AND FOUNTAINS

Reflecting Pool is a tree-lined vista. The 1-acre pool clearly reflects the entire vista when the 157 jets in the 40-foot-diameter ring are turned off. Five and a half feet deep at the deepest section, the pool takes three days to fill and holds 750,000 gallons of water. When the jets are on, which is most of the time in season, it is a splendid sight.

The *Four Seasons* statues around the **Reflecting Pool** are sculpted in white carrara marble. The sculptor, Henri Crenier (1873–1948), combined classical mythology with Art Nouveau style. Facing the pool, the statues are *Spring* on the far left, *Summer* on the left, *Fall* on the right, and *Winter* on the far right.

In classical mythology, two of the four seasons of the year were female and two were male. The original characters were Spring and Summer, female, and Winter and Fall, male. But Crenier made Summer male and Fall female. He maintained several of the symbols associated with the mythological gods and goddesses: Summer with garment cast aside, Fall with grapes, and Winter with wind blowing.

Beyond the pool is the Maze Garden, in front of the Colonnade. Canadian hemlocks form the main hedges of the maze, and the inner hedges are of Helleri holly. The trees lining the Maze Garden have been cubed to create a formal setting. The entire garden is tilted so that the pattern can be seen from the mansion. In the center of this beautiful garden is **Achievement,** another spectacular fountain by Crenier. Triton, a merman, is sculpted in white carrara marble. The face of Neptune, King of the Oceans, is on each side of the base. The center statue is bronze and was originally gold leaf; currently it is painted gold.

The Maze Garden leads to the Colonnade, designed by Thomas Hastings and built in 1926 as a memorial to Pierre-Samuel du Pont de Nemours. Past the Colonnade are the **Sunken Gardens,** designed by Alfred Victor du Pont (the son of Alfred I. du Pont) and Gabriel Massena, and constructed between 1928 and 1932. The walls and steps are of travertine from Rome. The statuary is white carrara marble.

The main statuary at the top and the side statues in the fountains, which are breathtaking, were sculpted in 1930 by Charles Sarrabezolles (c. 1888–

▼ SUNKEN GARDENS FOUNTAINS

1971). He was primarily a religious sculptor, which may account for the fact that two of the figures in the main statuary group of the Sunken Gardens look like putti-small angels. The bronzes in the pool and the wall fountains along the side of the gardens are the work of Claude Grange (c. 1890–1971).

Grottoes were considered to look like vestiges of the Roman bath. Throughout the gardens, a grotto motif recurs, similar to water dripping down a cave wall of the volcano rock tufa used in Italian grottoes. The niche areas in the side fountains at the Colonnade and in the Sunken Gardens are also reminiscent of Roman styling.

This is a trip not to be missed by any lover of gardens and fountains. You will feel as though you are visiting the chateau region of France. The Sunken Gardens and their fountains alone are worth the visit. For information, tour reservations, and directions, call Nemours at 800-651-6912.

Bibliography

Bach, Penny Balkin. *Public Art in Philadelphia*. Philadelphia: Temple University Press, 1992.

Cremer, Jill. "The History and Conservation of 19th and Early 20th Century Drinking Fountains in Philadelphia's Fairmount Park." Master's thesis, Graduate School of Architecture, Planning and Preservation, Columbia University, 1996. Courtesy Fairmount Park Commission Archives.

Fairmount Park Historic Preservation Trust. "Frederick Graff Memorial Fairmount Water Works, Documentation and Conservation Planning Report." December 1977.

———. "Water Works South Garden: Conditions Assessment and Treatment Recommendations." June 1999.

Finkel, Kenneth. *Philadelphia Then and Now*. Philadelphia: Library Company of Philadelphia, 1988.

Gibson, Jane. *The Fairmount Waterworks Bulletin*. Philadelphia Museum of Art, 1988.

Harris, Mary Virginia. *A Very Special Building: The University Museum*. Philadelphia: University Museum, 1983.

Klein, William M., Jr. *Gardens of Philadelphia and the Delaware Valley*. Philadelphia: Temple University Press, 1995.

Marion, John Francis. *Bicentennial City*. Princeton, NJ: Pyne Press, 1974.

Nemours Foundation. Nemours Mansion and Gardens. Nemours Foundation, 1999.

Philadelphia: Fairmount Park Art Association. *Sculpture of a City: Philadelphia's Treasure in Bronze and Stone*. New York: Walker Publishing Company, 1974.

Philadelphia: Three Centuries of American Art. Catalog. Philadelphia: Philadelphia Museum of Art, 1976.

Randall, Colvin. *Longwood Gardens*. Wilmington, DE: Longwood Gardens, 1992.

Scharf, Thomas J., and Thompson Westcott. *History of Philadelphia 1609–1884*, vol. 3. Philadelphia: L. H. Everets & Co., 1884.

Silverman, Sharon Hernes. *Brandywine Valley: The Informed Traveler's Guide*. Mechanicsburg, PA: Stackpole Books, 2004.

Strahan, Edward, ed. *A Century After: Picturesque Glimpses of Philadelphia and Pennsylvania*. Philadelphia: Allen, Lane & Scott, 1875.

Vogel, Morris J. *Cultural Connections*. Philadelphia: Temple University Press, 1991.

Webster, Richard. *Philadelphia Preserved*. Philadelphia: Temple University Press, 1976.

Weigley, Russell F., ed. *Philadelphia: A 300-Year History*. New York: W. W. Norton and the Barra Foundation, 1982.